# Up, Up, and Away

by Ellen Catala

Consultant: James R. Hipp, Ray S. Miller Army Airfield Operations Officer, Minnesota Army National Guard, Camp Ripley

Yellow Umbrella Books
for early readers

Yellow Umbrella Books are published by Red Brick Learning
7825 Telegraph Road, Bloomington, Minnesota 55438
http://www.redbricklearning.com

Editorial Director: Mary Lindeen
Senior Editor: Hollie J. Endres
Senior Designer: Gene Bentdahl
Photo Researcher: Signature Design
Developer: Raindrop Publishing
Consultant: James R. Hipp, Ray S. Miller Army Airfield Operations Officer,
  Minnesota Army National Guard, Camp Ripley
Conversion Assistants: Jenny Marks, Laura Manthe

*Library of Congress Cataloging-in-Publication Data*
Catala, Ellen
  Up, Up, and Away / by Ellen Catala
      p. cm.
  Includes index.
  ISBN 0-7368-5835-0 (hardcover)
  ISBN 0-7368-5265-4 (softcover)
  1. Flying machines—Juvenile literature. 2. Airplanes—Juvenile literature. I. Title. II. Series.
  TL600.C38 2005
  629.133—dc22
                                    2005016153

Photo Credits:
Cover–Page 2: Jupiter Images; Pages 3 and 4: Bettmann/Corbis; Page 5: Hulton-Deutsch
Collection/Corbis; Page 6: Time & Life Pictures/Getty Images, Inc.; Page 7: Time & Life
Pictures/Getty Images Inc.; Pages 8 and 9: Bettmann/Corbis; Page 10: Museum of
Flight/Corbis; Page 11: Bettmann/Corbis; Pages 12 and 13: Jupiter Images; Page 14: Corel

1 2 3 4 5 6 11 10 09 08 07 06

# Table of Contents

# Early Flying Machines

Have you ever seen a bird or a butterfly and wished you could fly? If you have, then you know why people **invented** flying machines.

The first flying machines were kites. Kites were invented in China many centuries ago. Kites were pretty as they soared through the air, but they could not carry people.

Some people tried attaching wings to their arms. They flapped and flapped but could not get off the ground. Others designed fancy flying machines, but these did not work either.

# Hot Air Balloons

Two French brothers invented the **hot air balloon**. They got the idea while watching scraps of paper being lifted by the hot air of a fireplace.

# Gliders

People loved hot air balloons, but they wanted to do more than float on the breeze. They noticed that birds sometimes soared. This sparked a new idea—the **glider**.

Early gliders let people fly in a certain direction, but the gliders were dangerous. Sometimes they stayed up, but most of the time they crashed! People wanted a better flying machine.

# The First Airplane

Then came two brothers, Orville and Wilbur Wright, who owned a bicycle shop. The Wright brothers liked building machines. They were also very interested in flying.

The Wright brothers started by building gliders. First, they attached wires to the wings for steering. Then they added an engine they built to power their glider.

One cold December day in 1903, the
Wright brothers tried their new flying
machine. It was called the Wright Flyer,
and it was the very first **airplane**. The
Wright Flyer stayed up for 12 seconds.

# Helicopters, Jets, and Beyond

Those 12 seconds changed everything.

Now people could really fly. What would come next? Over the next 50 years or so, many different flying machines were invented.

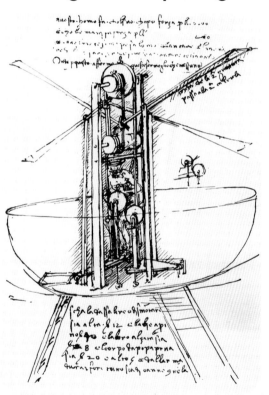

The **helicopter** was one of those
inventions. It flew like a hummingbird.
The helicopter could lift straight up off
the ground, and it could even move
backwards! This made it perfect for
rescue missions.

The **jet plane** was another invention. It was like an ordinary airplane, but it had special engines that let it move very fast. Now people could travel more quickly.

No longer do people just wish they could fly—they really can! Thanks to the invention of the rocket, people can even fly to the moon and beyond. Up, up, and away . . . .

# Glossary

**airplane**—a flying machine with an engine and wings

**glider**—a flying machine with wings and no engine

**helicopter**—a flying machine with propellers on the top and tail on the back

**hot air balloon**—a flying machine with a large fabric balloon that is filled with hot air; it has a basket below to carry passengers.

**invent**—to make something new based on an original idea

**jet plane**—an airplane with an engine that pushes air backward to move the plane forward

# Index

Word Count: 376
Early-Intervention Level: L